AF580246

SORROWS OF SERENDIPITY

NAISHA
CHANDRA

First published by Naisha Chandra in 2023

Table of Contents

Healing

DEDICATION

To all the untold tales
And the ones with missing details
I'm here to tell a story
Where love stands tall in all its glory...

FALLING

FIRST FALL

When I saw your back
I knew it's all I had to know
To let myself wander on the uncharted track
And to fill my heart with, "No".

It was the time you looked up
When I watched you watch the wall
That I saw something which was enough
To inevitably make me fall.

I stood by, hunching my shoulders
Waited for your visionary call
It didn't occur to me until it was over
That all I did was hopefully bawl.

Told myself it was all fate
Written in that sinister star
It never led to a place of hate
Instead, I taught myself to love you from afar.

MOON

Perhaps you're like the moon
Blotched, bruised and blemished
Needing something else to gleam
Needing to conceal behind darkness when it's your turn to beam

Perhaps you're like the moon
Your image in the water lies to me
Your secrets spilling out of you
Like you won't disappear and go to someone new

Perhaps you're like the moon
All your phases are loved by your light
Stars align themselves when you're blue
But your beauty never fades, even if you do

Perhaps you are the moon
You shall need a sun to shine
Maybe I'll burn myself to become one
And maybe burn everyone else and keep you shunned.

INTIMACY

Holding your breath when they're away
Stroking the back of their hand when they stay
Untangling their incongruous necklace
Laying with them in their beautiful mess

Leaving little notes in their favourite books
They read them while you read all their looks
Painting them pink when they're blue
Always looking at them while they look at the
view

Putting yourself between them and the cars
Counting their freckles while they count the
stars
They hold your heart as you hold their hand
Your eyes were something only they
could ever understand

DREAM

I said, "They break me,"
You said, "I'll break with you."
I said, "They hate me,"
You said, "I'll hate them for you."

You wrote letters for me in the summer
Made hearts from leaves in autumn and spring
Sculpted my face in snow in the winter
Stayed with me in the rain on the swing

I asked, "How could you love me?"
You said, "I fear there's no one like you."
I asked, "Would you ever leave me?"
You said, "Life is too fearful to live without you."

You promised to dance with me in my dream
But I couldn't sleep the entire night
So, you danced with me beside a stream
Making everything seem like it's right

I asked, "Could you find a home in me?"
You said, "You're all I find at the end of every road."
I asked, "Did you find your soul in me?"
You said, "I am you, heart and hope."

ALWAYS

I'd wanted to be found
Maybe that's why I always hid
But everything swirled when you were around
So I always won and you never did

The colours merged into white
While all faded to black
I couldn't look away, even if I tried
Always found the light in the crack

You loved me like rain
Soothing me everywhere at once
Wasn't something we could ever explain
Like the droplets always running through our pulse

Our kisses were a brush of bizarre art
Where all our worries subside
Two spirits igniting a sacred spark
Always burning the places I hide.

COLOURS OF THE GALAXY

I asked and got it
Everything that I've ever wanted
From the shooting stars and from you
From the Neptune who only gave me blue

Your eyes had the darkness of grey
Just like Mercury in the milky way
Burning into me like the sun
Making us both come undone

Your body was striped and tan
As if Jupiter was reborn as a man
It kept me grounded to the core
Just like the Earth did to the blue-green shore

The Saturn had everything
Just like me with your golden ring
And the gift of moons
The one you gave, promising me all your Junes.

LITTLE THINGS

It's your hand in my hair
And on my skin when it's bare
It's the look in your eyes
When we share the same air

Mayhap it's the colour on your face
Or the lack of space
Which makes me shiver
Bruising with a soul crushing embrace

Maybe it's not the flower laden shore
Just you opening my car's door
It's only the littlest things
Which is worth loving you more.

DETAILS

It’s the tiniest details
How staining broken glasses
Could be so very beautiful
Contrary to the chip in my nails
To the stale smelling cocktails
And to the improbable fairy tales.
How everything I'm made of
Reeks of you and your cologne
And the soft gentle touch of your fingers.
It's the tiniest details
Of how your eyes shine in the sun
How your skin glows
And how you blush as if you'd been out for a run.
I found myself inside of you
Yet was afraid to look
Afraid, if I looked too far and deep
I'll find the tiniest details
Which will be enough to make me leave.

SHATTERING

BLUE LILY

Black scribble lines, crowd my mind
Like being stuck in a cobweb
Like a mouse in a trap
Like the sun shining so bright, you're suddenly, indefinitely, blind.

Eyes closing involuntarily,
Seeing nothing, but looking for everything at once
Tired of it in a revolution, limp and hunched,
Like a wilted, dark, blue lily.

Music sounded like melancholia,
Wine tasted like love
Nothing could've warned me about,
How love didn't exist beyond dystopia.

Should've wept and wailed and wronged,
If I knew the moon would one day haunt me
The way my mind did, and
The way my gilded self never belonged.

AUGUST

Hoped we'd go in the rain together
Holding hands, nothing but tears in between
Touch as light as a feather
Making it nothing but a daydream

You wanted to flee, but I did instead
Solvating all my Monday blues
As Taylor once said
"You weren't mine to lose"

WOULD YOU HAVE?

I must've made a mistake,
Thinking you'd ever count the stars with me.
Would you have ever liked me back,
If I never asked you to see what I could see.

'The jokes we shared began to fade,
All because you were beautiful and I was a disgrace.
Would you have ever liked me back,
If I tried to love you in the first place?'

Time floated in the sky,
As I was marooned in the depth of your eyes.
Would you have ever liked me back?
If I let you hear every single one of my cries.

'It hurt me to laugh at the ocean of thoughts you spilled,
Our voices mixing in a blur.
Would you have ever liked me back,
If I never loved her?'

ME AND YOU

Fine dine, spilled wine
Me and you, black & white
Bitter sweet, freezing heat
Me and you, a distorted beat

Blunt words, sharp pain
Me and you, loved to hate
Noticed her, overlooked him
Me and you, strongly limped

Beautiful memories, ugly pictures
Me and you, died to live
Cold as him, warm as her
Me and you, a distinct blur

Night and day, Moon and Sun
Me and you, never learn
Better or for worse
Me and you, were never meant to work.

TRAGEDY

His touch was now burning holes
Into my ashen soul
Where resides all his other touches
Which never used to be this cruel or cold

I used to drown in his eyes
Caught my breath every time
But now I gasp for air
Every time he lies

My heart used to be so full
It was almost beautiful
But then it broke
And the hollowness is almost awful

He turned quiet into a crowd
Tore me to bits without a sound
Made me believe I was culpable
When he was the tragedy without a doubt.

REVERIE

I don't know myself; I don't know who I am,
I just know it's not enough to not be a lamb.
Bring me flowers, bring me hope
It's almost blinding to see myself gnaw and grope.

I don't want to feel how I cry most nights,
I just want to fly to the vultures in those heights.
High hugs, klutzy kisses, crippling cuddles,
Maybe I'll find solace in those paltry puddles.

Caressing, caring, cooing turns into,
Battling, bawling and booing.
Mountains hear the echo of my heartbeat,
Until my dried tears are all I've left to eat.

Crushes crushed, Howling’s hushed,
But I don't stop until I'm touched.
Roses are red, violets are blue,
Until everything's a lie and nothing's the truth.

I don't want to hear the defeated sighs,
Just give me back my deafening cries.
I would rather be known for my misery and treachery,
Than be known for my foolish love and this broken reverie.

ARDOR OF ELEMENTS

The way the sea asked me
If I ever drowned in the sky,
The moon answered on my behalf,
"The stars heard all her cries."

The trees stirred awake
With the deafening breeze, blowing away from my wails
The sun whispered softly,
"Did you ever feel like a blaze?"

Maybe the snow understood,
What it's like to be blue
The thunder roared quietly,
"Did he ever love you the way we do?"

THE LAST OF IT

All the messages I sent
All the memories I kept
Safe in my life, safe in my heart
Writing letters among the tainted stars

Oh, how beautiful your soul
How soulful your eyes
And haunting, horrible heart crying inside of me
How I pity those who cannot see and shine

See YOU, and everything inside
Can't look at your profound claws
Digging at the taunting walls
Where I wept and wept and cried

Every touch laced with regret and sorrow
Pulled apart my bones that were endlessly hollow
You made me believe that colouring inside the tarnished lines
Never got me whatever was ever mine.

HEALING

LAST DANCE

Held your shoulder for the last time
It felt like my soul had come alive
Sparks lit up around our heads
Until all I could smell was thyme

Your hand was calloused, mine was cold
They fit like it was meant for us to hold
We moved to the rhythm of our tale
The one that would forever remain untold

You pledge to never look into my eyes
After all our movement dies
I promised to never look into yours
Until we find some other and time flies

Our foreheads meet, halfway through our romance
Hearts finally feeling like a lance
Traced the tears burning down our faces
Branding them in our skin, along
with our last dance.

NEVER WAS

We fell like snow
Light and low
But when we froze
And I slipped
You severed our symphonic souls.

The candle melted
Dull and dejected
But when I put it out
And darkened all our nights
You never made a sound.

Count the clouds
Find me in the crowds
When you finally pause
And I'm not there
You could finally let go of what never was.

SORROWS OF SERENDIPTIY

By staying close to you
I learnt how to stay away
How to not listen to you
But still be near you in dismay

The end of your happiness
Gave way to my peace
The void full of blackness
Welcomed me with ease

The uncertainty of blood moon
Shone the ambiguity of you
Snow in the month of June
Suddenly seemed believable than the truth

Spiralling down a path of broken glass
Seemed a fitting possibility
Than seeing the indentations of you in the grass
Without hindering with my tranquillity

Years of hopelessness
Led to this moment of vulnerability
It never occurred to me when this loathsomeness
Altered into sorrows of serendipity

WASN'T LOVE

It started with me saying "I do"
Making me laugh when you said me too.
Didn't realise it wasn't love,
Until you started calling me a bluff.

Waking up to an empty bed every day,
Always thought you wanted to stay.
Didn't realise it wasn't love,
Until you flew to heaven and above.

I thought I was mad,
That you took everything I had.
Didn't realise it wasn't love,
Until I was glad that you were a dove.

You said, “love me more when I'm dead",
Now I want nothing more than to get rid of your head.
Didn't realise it wasn't love,
Until you broke me and I had enough.

Sitting beside your grave,
Thinking to myself, 'was I your slave?'
Didn't realise it wasn't love,
Until our marriage was pure fluff.

But now I was content,
Not bothered about the time I had spent.
Didn't realise it wasn't love,
Until I had started over at dusk.

SEASON CHANGED

The wind flew away
All those dead leaves and love
Which you crunched and killed
To an area which was grey
To a place where I never prayed
And to a scene where we first lay,
In the heat of the summer
And of our hearts
You burned the rest of us
Like ill-fated lovers
But I never told another
And removed all your colours,
Gonna love myself more this September
Because you never did
And autumn doesn't deserve it
You won't be here to remember
All through May to December
My skin would glow like embers.

EPIPHANY

I had an epiphany,
That you were always hearing but never listened
That you were always looking but never saw
Saw something I was holding on to forever
The kind of forever you see in movies
The kind of forever you see in law
The kind I was willing to give up for you
I smiled when you did and screamed when you were blue
But never once did I ask for anything that wasn't you
I could run but you'd never stop me
I could fly but you'd let me leave
I would rather go live somewhere far away
Than to see you walk away
Truly, it's incongruous to stand next you
When all you stood for was anything but the reality of me
And that's when I was ready
To expunge you
And to see your moment of epiphany.

CAPITULATE

She swam until she sunk
She drank until she was drunk
Exhaled until there wasn't any air left
Lost until she knew she wasn't the best.

Shattered herself into a million hearts
Still loathed all of those parts
Yet loved with each one
Just like the moon loved the sun.

Warmth radiated from her, by her, through her
But never to her
She flew as far as she could, as high as possible
Just so the birds would become inaudible

Sometimes there's nowhere to go, to run, to stay
When the nights suddenly become days
When the clouds creep up on her
She stops breaking, and starts breathing.

FIXED

Trees so benevolent
Eyes so transcendent
Rivers flowing so fast
That my heart never caught up,
My feet did instead and I reached the shore
Listened to the waves' burning roar
Tried to fix the miserable, broken oar
But it ended up being a worthless chore.
So I fixed my fragmented heart
The one that drowned an eternity ago
The one I never let go
And the one where love for you only grows.
In the depths where our souls entwined
I swore to never come up for air
But now when I'm finally breathing,
I broke the thread where I was confined.

EPILOGUE

I want to ruin myself in the beauty of words
Drown myself in the ink that presents them
I want no one to lay eyes on these words
Make everyone burn in the serenity of them

I want to reel in the wrath of words
Pretend to be bewitched by them
I want to be pleased by these words
Never let them know the power they hold in them

I want to not feel the urgency of words
Wanting to be consumed by them
I want to graze these words
Like I never want to be apart from them

I want to caress the vulnerability of words
Collect every stray tear shed by them
I want a promise of forever by these words
Trying to beg and break them

I want to keep the everlasting love of words
Scent of desire and despair left by them
I want to bottle the lingering touch of these words
Sleep in the indentation marked by them.

ACKNOWLEDGMENT

Whaaatttt?? This is so new. And there are plenty of people who helped me navigate this new journey and I am grateful to all of them.

First and foremost, the most important person, who was there with me from the birth of this book's idea till this very moment, who read all my poems the very minute I wrote them, who helped me to not burst into tears every time I wanted to throw something away, who gave me her objective opinions on all the illustrations without laughing, and without whom this book probably wouldn't even exist, Ritvee Budhiraja, thank you for teaching me how to use Word without pulling out my hair, and I appreciate all your unconditional support and love. I love you so much.

Thank you, Mom and Dad and Nabhya, my little baby sister, for letting me take away some of our precious family time to plan this book and being my rock.

Shreya and Vrinda, I love you for just being there and becoming the break I sometimes needed desperately and keeping me in check. Love you girlies.

Last but not the least, thank you to all those who stuck with me from my initial Wattpad days and are still here, reading the things I write and loving me.

I love you all.

Beautiful things are coming.

I am such an author.

www.ingramcontent.com/pod-product-compliance
Lightning Source LLC
LaVergne TN
LVHW070257170826
845679LV00030B/1401

9798891861282